First Edition

This workbook is dedicated to all
the seekers, to those who love to
dig just a little deeper. Keep digging!

ISBN-10: 0692306080
ISBN-13: 978-0692306086

Design and layout by Nicki Drumb & Rachel Gardiner.

Quotes by Napoleon Hill used by permission from the Napoleon Hill Foundation. www.NapHill.org
Quote by Rhonda Byrne used by permission. www.thesecret.tv

Contents

Acknowledgments

Thank you to Claude Bristol for sharing what he knew with the rest of us; and for all the other teachers who do the same. I love this stuff!

I am forever thankful for the Global Information Network's founders, speakers, members and friends. One of the best choices I ever made was getting involved with that group. Thank you to all of you for the endless encouragement, belief, information and getting me dreaming again!

Many, many thanks to Nicki Drumb and Rachel Gardiner who literally made this book happen. I'm thankful for you on so many levels, SO THANKFUL!!

Thank you to my family for absolutely everything.

To Melissa Rosario, thank you for being such a strong example of what it means to put passion and commitment into life, love and work. You inspire me endlessly! You're my favorite.

FOREWORD

by

ED FOREMAN

This workbook, masterfully and lovingly prepared by Rebekah Keyes, will help you to discover, understand, and utilize the wondrous and magnificent power of *Believing!* Only a unique few will take the time to evaluate, comprehend, and implement this *MAGIC* into their lives!

First, you must read… not just scan… but slowly, thoughtfully, and deliberately read, study, feel, and experience Claude Bristol's magnificent book, *The Magic of Believing,* an all-time bestseller that is as current, useful and meaningful today as when it was first written… and as it will continue to be a century from now!

The Magic of Believing ranks right up there with the best self-help books ever written… i.e., *Think and Grow Rich* by Napoleon Hill; *Psycho-Cybernetics* by Maxwell Maltz; *The Power of Your Subconscious Mind* by Joe Murphy; *The Power of Positive Thinking* by Dr. Norman Vincent Peale; *How to Win Friends and Influence* People by Dale Carnegie; *Man's Search for Meaning* by Dr. Viktor Frankl; *What to Say When You Talk to Yourself* by Shad Helmstetter; *Power Vs. Force* by David Hawkins; and *The Bible.* If you have only these ten books in your library and regularly apply their lessons in your life, you will enjoy health, happiness, success, and longevity!

For almost a half century, I've been privileged to teach our SUCCESSFUL LIFE Course principles based upon the lessons in these books and the resulting experiences making up my incredibly happy, healthy, enjoyable, and prosperous life. The careful, thoughtful completion of the exercises in this Workbook will boost you along your path to a happier, healthier, more *SUCCESSFUL life.* Best wishes to you on a Magical Journey.

Ed Foreman, U. S Congressman (Rtd.)
Texas and New Mexico
Speaker, Author, Entrepreneur

Shovel, Spoon or Backhoe

This is where the digging begins! You are obviously on a journey; you are a seeker seeking, what? What's the reason you've picked up this workbook to *The Magic of Believing*?

Most of us are seeking something; it's a little different for everyone and yet largely similar. We want success, however we define it. We want happiness, understanding, abundance, quality relationships, trust, financial security, great health, joyful experiences; we want this life to be as fun, fulfilling and rewarding as it can be. We want to express ourselves, we want to contribute, and we want to be part of something bigger.

Can this workbook help you on your journey? It's really up to you. This workbook is like most everything else in that you'll get as much out of it as you put in. Things only work and work best when you work them. *The Magic of Believing* is an incredible book with success principles and insights that can help anyone get where they want to go. However, we sometimes read too quickly; we skim over deeper meanings; we fail to integrate what we're learning into our everyday lives. When we do that, we miss the whole point. This book wasn't intended just to be read and placed aside. It was meant to be applied, and *experienced*. In this way you'll create a deeper understanding, you'll integrate the information into your daily life and THAT will change everything.

Whether or not you've read *The Magic of Believing* before doesn't matter. You're at the perfect place to begin! I would recommend that you read each chapter once through, and twice is better, before going through the corresponding chapter in the workbook. (As a side note, the questions in each workbook's chapter run chronologically with the unfolding of the chapter in the book for ease of reference.)

Here are a few guidelines as you begin:

- As you are reading, when you come across a word you don't know, stop and look it up in the dictionary. Not doing so will cause you to miss some vital point or understanding.

- The 'Fill in the Blank' questions are direct quotes from the book.

- There are some 'Bonus' questions or activities to do. I highly recommend that you do them in order to further engage your own evolving thought process and ideas. You may come across some more dramatic "ah-ha!" moments in this way.

- Don't feel hindered by the amount of lines following a question. If you have more to say, say it! Keep some extra sheets of paper around or tucked into your workbook and keep on writing!

Shovel, spoon or backhoe? You decide which tool you use and how deep you go by your level of participation. This is YOUR workbook and there's no due date. Take the time to look deeply, to think deeply, and to participate in the process.

Rebekah Keyes

January 11, 2014

"I didn't get my start until I was 37.
It was very, very difficult for me. I had
a frequently unemployed husband and
a house full of kids. My first advice to
anyone is to read *The Magic of Believing*.
It changed my life.

Read it and absorb the ideas that he puts
forth in the book. You won't even think
of your age or the obstacles in your way;
you'll think of your dream, and how to
keep focused on your dream."

Phyllis Diller

INTRODUCTION

by

EARLENE VINING

Rebekah Keyes was a very dynamic participant in the 3-day SUCCESSFUL LIFE Course which Ed Foreman and I teach several times a year at various locations in the U.S.A. and Europe. Most of our U.S. classes are conducted at the beautiful McCormick's Creek State Park in Spencer, Indiana, where Rebekah attended. During those three days with her, it was obvious that Rebekah is a student of success principles and not afraid to Dream Big Dreams!

The fact that you are utilizing this workbook makes you a member of a very select group of winners who are in pursuit of personal growth… Congratulations!

The Magic of Believing, by Claude Bristol, has been an integral part of my ability to resist negativity while pursuing my goals. I have reviewed the book at least once a year for the past 30 years. It is my opinion that it should be a part of the curriculum in every high school and University. God gave us a supreme intelligence that helps direct our ability to make choices that influence our destiny. It is up to us to have the courage to activate that intelligence and inner wisdom to achieve happiness and success.

Rebekah's workbook will help you to identify and define what is keeping you from overcoming obstacles that may be interfering with your belief system. Perhaps one of life's most difficult challenges is to **let go of the past, accept where you are, and invite, expect, and visualize a successful future of health, wealth and happiness.** *The Magic of Believing* contains all the principles necessary to help you achieve your highest potential, and this Workbook is the catalyst to make it happen!

Studying and completing this great workbook will help get you where you want to go, armed with a renewed belief system, an elevated confidence, enriched self-esteem, and an abundance of energy! Life is a magical journey. You are here to experience and enjoy it!

Rebekah, I am honored that you asked me to write this Introduction. Your workbook is and will be a great blessing to all those who are fortunate enough to discover and utilize it!

Earlene Vining
Speaker, Author, Entrepreneur, Mother of Three

"Our life is shaped by our mind; we become what we think. Suffering follows an evil thought as the wheels of a cart follow the oxen that draw it.

Our life is shaped by our mind; we become what we think. Joy follows a pure thought like a shadow that never leaves."

The Dhammapada, verses 1 & 2

Chapter 1
How I came to tap the power of belief

"If you think you can or think you can't,
either way you're right. It's the thinking
that makes it so."

Henry Ford

Chapter 1. How I came to tap the power of belief

1. What have I experienced or heard about, "miracle" or otherwise, that has caused me to wonder and ask questions?

    _____

    _____

    _____

2. What spiritual, religious or personal experiences have I had that reflect the author's experiences?

    _____

    _____

    _____

3. The author researched many philosophies, sects and ideas. What new ways of thinking or believing have I investigated?

    _____

    _____

    _____

4. Identify something I believe, with or without proof or evidence. It could be something I've chosen to believe on faith, or something I believe without ever really questioning or examining it — a postulate.

    _____

    _____

    _____

5. "The forces I had unconsciously set in motion were already setting the stage for me." Recall a time when I made a decision that seemed to carry itself to completion through me, almost of its own accord.

    _____

    _____

    _____

    _____

6. Where in my own life have I seen instances of an unknown force, or luck, at work? What about lately?

_____

_____

_____

7. When I think of my future, what pictures do I see? What sorts of scenarios do I play out in my mind?

_____

_____

_____

8. How do I define or describe 'coincidence'?

_____

_____

_____

9. Fill in the blanks: "You have often heard it said that you can ____ _____ _____ you can."

10. Research and describe the placebo effect. List a few examples.

_____

_____

_____

11. The author speaks of medical and other types of specialists who resist any new ideas, research or theories that contradict what they already think and believe. In what ways and areas am I a 'specialist,' resisting new information?

_____

_____

_____

12. Are my beliefs frozen or open to adjustment?

_____

_____

_____

_____

13. "Persistence gives confidence and continued right mental attitude followed by consistent action will bring success. I know the formula that leads to the fullest success. When you have that knowing *inside* you, fear vanishes, as do the obstructions to a continued life of all good." What do I think of this statement?

_____

_____

_____

Bonus: read *TNT- It Rocks the Earth,* by Claude Bristol. Thoughts:

_____

_____

_____

14. Fill in the Blank:

"With our own _____ of ruin, we were attracting the disaster to ourselves."

15. It's not what's happening around me, it's my "mental attitude" towards it. To what in my life currently can I apply this statement?

_____

_____

_____

16. What other thoughts or experiences did I have while reading this chapter?

_____

_____

_____

_____

_____

_____

_____

_____

_____

_____

Chapter 2
Mind-stuff Experiments

"Mind is the Master power that molds and makes,
And Man is Mind, and evermore he takes
The tool of Thought, and, shaping what he wills,
Brings forth a thousand joys, a thousand ills.
He thinks in secret, and it comes to pass:
Environment is but his looking glass."

James Allen, *As a Man Thinketh*

Chapter 2. Mind-stuff experiments

1. Fill in the Blank:

    "Your very life is your _____ - and the result of your _____ _____. It is your mind and what you think that makes you what you _____."

2. How do I see my habits of thought, my patterns of thinking, reflected in my life?

    _____

    _____

    _____

3. What does my attitude say about me?

    _____

    _____

    _____

4. The way I present myself, my dress, appearance, hygiene, grooming, my manners – what does it say about my thought patterns?

    _____

    _____

    _____

5. How do the people I choose as friends reflect my thinking habits?

    _____

    _____

    _____

6. What does the way I walk say about me?

    _____

    _____

    _____

7. What are some more examples of the outward evidence of my habitual thoughts?

    _____

    _____

    _____

8. The author says, "What you *believe* yourself to be, you are." Who do I believe myself to be? What kind of person?

_____

_____

_____

Bonus: Research and find Earl Nightingale's *The Strangest Secret* audio. Listen to it. Have I heard it before? Listen again. Thoughts:

_____

_____

_____

9. How would I describe the law of cause and effect as it applies to the operation of the mind?

_____

_____

_____

10. Thomas Edison said that, "Ideas come from space." Have I ever experienced a new idea to seemingly "come from space" into my mind?

_____

_____

_____

11. How do I interpret and understand what Paracelsus said about faith?

_____

_____

12. Think of someone I know who works a lot and never seems to get ahead. Think of someone I know who seems to succeed easily. Analyze and compare their attitudes.

_____

_____

_____

13. Fill in the Blank: "The successful people in history have succeeded through their _____."

14. What do I think of that statement?

_____

_____

_____

_____

15. Remember a time when I was absolutely and singly focused on something – and got what I was after. What was it like?

_____

_____

_____

16. I must know what I want. What is my goal, exactly?

_____

_____

_____

_____

17. Have I visualized what I really want? How often?

_____

_____

18. If my goal is financial, what amount? If achievement, what specifically? If a relationship, what kind of person? Write it out!

_____

_____

_____

_____

_____

_____

_____

_____

"All that we are is the result of what we have thought."

Buddha

19. On a scale from 1 to 10, how bad do I want it? (1 being a little, 10 being a great deal.)

1-------------2-------------3-------------4-------------5-------------6-------------7-------------8-------------9-------------10

20. On a scale from 1 to 10, how focused am I? (1 being a little, 10 being a great deal.)

1-------------2-------------3-------------4-------------5-------------6-------------7-------------8-------------9-------------10

Bonus: Dig into psychokinesis and research contemporary experimentation for evidence. What did I find? Thoughts:

_____

_____

_____

_____

_____

_____

_____

_____

_____

21. The author says, "No matter what the character of your thoughts, they do create after their kind. When this sinks into your consciousness, you get some inkling of the awe-inspiring power which is yours to use." Think about this for a minute or two. What does this mean to me?

_____

_____

_____

_____

_____

_____

_____

Bonus: Dig into the idea of auras and energy by researching Kirlian photo images. What did I see? What do I think?

_____

_____

_____

"The subconscious mind may be likened to a magnet, and when it has been vitalized and thoroughly saturated with any definite purpose, it has a decided tendency to attract all that is necessary for the fulfillment of that purpose. Like attracts like, and you may see evidence of this law in every blade of grass and every growing tree."

Napoleon Hill,
The Law of Success in 16 Lessons

22. Dig deep into Pythagoras' theory of vibration. Research it. What did I learn?

_____

_____

_____

_____

23. The author cites some examples of vibration in every day occurrences: water into steam and my five senses interpreting the frequencies of sight, sound, and smell. Have I ever thought of it this way before? Think about tuning a radio into a particular frequency for my favorite radio station; think about dialing a number to reach a particular person on my cell phone. How does it work?

_____

_____

_____

_____

24. Do the needle and paper experiment. Remember that it takes "a little practice and confident and concentrated thinking." What did I experience?

_____

_____

_____

_____

25. How long can I really concentrate?

_____

_____

26. How could I learn to use this power and habit of concentration to my benefit?

_____

_____

_____

27. Do I pray, meditate, and/or visualize?

_____

_____

28. The author speaks at length of the power of belief. What do I believe?

_____

_____

_____

_____

_____

29. Another way to think of it is, What do I believe **in**?

_____

_____

_____

_____

_____

30. What do I believe so strongly that I feel _"charged with the vibrations of strong beliefs"_?

_____

_____

_____

_____

31. It can sometimes be a challenge to really get to the basis of what I believe because it's been combined with what other people believe, confused, or simply taken as "truth" or "fact".
For that reason, consider this:
What do I perceive as truth?
What basic assumptions do I make?
What do I usually expect to happen or experience?
What do I trust or count on enough to put the weight of my life on it?

_____

_____

_____

_____

_____

_____

32. How and where do I see evidence of my beliefs in my experience?

_____

_____

_____

_____

_____

_____

_____

_____

_____

33. What other thoughts or experiences did I have while reading this chapter?

_____

_____

_____

_____

_____

_____

_____

_____

_____

_____

_____

_____

_____

_____

"Just as the conscious mind is the source of thought, so the subconscious is the source of power."

Claude Bristol, *The Magic of Believing*

Chapter 3
What the Subconscious Really Is

Chapter 3. What the subconscious really is

1. The author talks about releasing a thought or situation from the conscious mind, only to have the solution or a new idea spring up later, or after sleeping and waking. Remember an instance when an answer or solution popped into my mind when I had changed my attention and was doing or thinking about something else entirely.

_____

_____

_____

_____

2. Remember a moment of inspiration which I acted on and it turned out to be the exact right thing to do.

_____

_____

_____

_____

3. Fill in the Blanks: "The subconscious mind is beyond space and time, and is fundamentally a powerful _____ and _____ station with a universal hookup."

4. The author makes it very clear that in order for the subconscious mind to accept and act upon a desire, I must SEE, IMAGINE and VISUALIZE myself as already successful. When I imagine myself as already successful, what do I see?

_____

_____

_____

_____

_____

_____

_____

5. Do I believe it's possible?

_____

_____

6. How big is my dream? Can I dream bigger?

_____

_____

_____

_____

7. The author says to wait patiently and with **absolute faith** for the subconscious to work out a plan or solution. Then, when the message is received by the conscious mind, to act on it right away. How do I receive messages from my subconscious?

_____

_____

_____

_____

8. What does "absolute faith" mean to me? How does it feel to operate with absolute faith?

_____

_____

_____

_____

9. Think of a time when a series of events or circumstances left me feeling confused, overwhelmed or some other generally negative feeling; however, on looking back, I could see how everything had worked out to my benefit.

_____

_____

_____

_____

10. Does this mean that the seemingly negative event or situation wasn't really negative at all? Does this apply to everything?

_____

_____

_____

_____

"You can do anything as long as you believe that you can. You can never have a dream without having a way to make it come true.

You have that dream and you hold that dream in your heart; you hold that dream in your vision; you passionately hold on to that vision and it is impossible for you to fail!

You *cannot* fail; you can only succeed, as long as you see your dream. The dream has to be bigger than you are. It's the journey of a lifetime! The larger this dream is, the bigger the changes you will experience in your life."

Peter Ragnar

11. Dream-building exercise! Let your imagination run. What would you do, have or be if money wasn't an object, time wasn't an issue, and you knew you couldn't fail.   **DREAM!!!**

_____

_____

_____

_____

_____

_____

_____

_____

_____

_____

_____

_____

_____

_____

_____

_____

_____

_____

_____

_____

_____

_____

_____

_____

_____

_____

_____

_____

_____

_____

_____

_____

_____

_____

_____

_____

_____

…get more paper; keep going!

12. What other thoughts or experiences did I have while reading this chapter?

_____

_____

_____

_____

_____

_____

_____

_____

_____

_____

_____

_____

_____

_____

_____

_____

"The subconscious mind accepts and acts on all suggestions that reach it, constructive or destructive, from your own mind or someone else's."

Napoleon Hill,
The Law of Success in 16 Lessons

Chapter 4
Suggestion is Power

"Faith is the substance of things hoped for,
the evidence of things not seen."

Hebrews 11:1

Chapter 4. Suggestion is Power

1. What is the dictionary definition of 'act'?

_____

_____

_____

2. Fill in the Blanks: "The power of suggestion – either autosuggestion (_____ _____
   _____ _____) or heterosuggestion (coming to you from _____ _____) –
   starts the machinery into operation, causing the subconscious mind to begin its creative work."

3. Think for a moment: what thoughts, beliefs or ideas do I repeat to myself frequently or
   throughout the day? Am I doing it consciously or unconsciously?

_____

_____

_____

4. What are some current examples of mass suggestion in more recent history? Consider media,
   politics, advertising, health care, religions, social justice...... What else? Keep considering.

_____

_____

_____

_____

5. Fill in the Blank: "Again we see the terrific force of _____ _____ – it is our master, and
   we do as we are ordered."

_____

_____

_____

_____

6. The author says, "only the things you become conscious of can harm or bother you." What do
   I think of this statement?

_____

_____

"Faith is the force of life."

Leo Tolstoy

Bonus: Read the book of James in the Bible. What does James say about faith?

_____

_____

_____

7. Knute Rockne, the great Notre Dame coach, was able to rouse, inspire, awaken and motivate his team to success. I can use this on myself! What are some thoughts, ideas, sayings or methods that I can encourage myself with?

_____

_____

_____

8. Now, write my own pep talk for when discouragement comes! Really get into the emotion of it; inspire, motivate and awaken **myself**!

_____

_____

_____

_____

9. I realize now that I can and do influence others through heterosuggestion. How have I been affecting those close to me? How do they affect me?

_____

_____

_____

10. If I would like my influence to be different, what can I do to change it?

_____

_____

11. The author says, "nothing comes into our economic sphere unless we first create it with our emotional thinking." How would I explain or describe 'emotional thinking'?

_____

_____

_____

_____

12. What are the three chief factors in developing the subconscious mind's magnetic forces?

_____

_____

_____

13. When I think of myself, my future, my success, my SELF, what do I see?

_____

_____

_____

14. Write about a time in my life where I focused on something, big or small, and the pieces seemed to come together "coincidentally".

_____

_____

_____

Bonus: Dig into Paracelsus; who was he and what did he think? Thoughts:

_____

_____

_____

_____

15. Doubts, fears, and negative thinking all get in the way of my success and happiness because they get in the way of my belief in myself. What are some specific doubts or fears that I have right now?

_____

_____

_____

_____

16. What is Unity City? What do they believe?

_____

_____

_____

_____

17. The author talks about concentrating through mental images on a desired result in order to consistently achieve that result. He cites golfers, pool players and Mr. Fillmore as saying, "If it works at all, it works everywhere."

In my life are there examples or instances where I hold mental pictures of specific outcomes and tend to experience those outcomes? It could be positive or negative, depending on the pictures or scenarios I most frequently play out in my mind.

In other words, what do I most often expect and therefore, most often *get*?

_____

_____

_____

_____

Bonus: Do the experiment of throwing stones at a tree or post. Really concentrate on creating and holding the mental picture of hitting your target. Have fun with it! What was my experience?

_____

_____

_____

18. "One will be a failure while the other will be the last word in culinary achievement. Why? In the first case, the one cook approaches pie-making with trepidation. She knows she has had pie failures in the past and worries how this one is going to come out. She doesn't have a perfect **mental picture** of an appetite-satisfying golden brown crust with a wonderful zestful filling. She's upset and nervous, and without her knowing it, her uneasiness is communicated to her pie-making. The second one is aware, she knows that her pie is going to be tops – and it is. That primary mental picture – her belief – makes it so." This is a perfect example of the outcomes I experience in life. Am I the first pie maker or the second one? Do I generally focus on past failures and worry how things will turn out?

_____

_____

_____

_____

_____

_____

"If you want to reach your goal, you must 'see the reaching' in your own mind before you actually arrive at your goal."

Zig Ziglar, *See You at the Top*

19. Am I aware of the mental pictures, the expectations, the beliefs that I hold?

_____

_____

_____

_____

_____

_____

_____

_____

_____

_____

20. What other thoughts or experiences did I have while reading this chapter?

_____

_____

_____

_____

_____

_____

_____

_____

_____

_____

"Logic will get you from A to B.
Imagination will take you everywhere."

Albert Einstein

Chapter 5
The Art of
Mental Pictures

Chapter 5. The Art of Mental Pictures

1. How do I perceive other people? Am I inferior, superior or equal?

_____

_____

2. What images or ideas do I hold of other people? How does this perception affect my relationships?

_____

_____

_____

3. Fill in the Blanks: "…for what we are _____ comes as the result of what we _____ _____."

4. What do I want? What am I working on or toward?

_____

_____

_____

5. For the next 2 to 5 minutes, sit quietly, eyes open or closed, and roll out a movie in my mind about the fulfillment of my dream – see it, feel it, live it as done. Take at least a good 2 to 5 minutes to really get into it. Where am I? What am I doing? Who is with me? How do I feel? What am I wearing? Make it vivid!

6. The author says that "fear is basically an imaginary factor". In other words, fear and worry is the misuse of my imagination. Worry is negative goal-setting. What do I think of these ideas? What is the opposite of worry?

_____

_____

_____

7. What are some things that I continually catch myself worrying about?

_____

_____

_____

_____

8. What is the placebo effect?

_____

_____

_____

9. Shakespeare said, "Assume a virtue if you have it not." In other words, imagine you have it, act like it, pretend. How much thought have I given to the kind of person I want to *be*, not just the stuff I want to have or experience? How much time spent visualizing myself as this person?

_____

_____

_____

Bonus: Dig deep into the history of Dr. Émile Coué. What did I learn?

_____

_____

_____

10. "When you employ your imagination properly, you see yourself doing a thing, and then you go ahead and do it." Action is the difference between wishful thinking and proper use of my imagination. What am I willing to DO to achieve my dreams?

_____

_____

_____

11. In the battles of imagination versus willpower, imagination always wins. What's an example of this phenomenon in my experience?

_____

_____

_____

12. The author says it's just as easy to shoot at a bird on a limb 30ft above the ground as it is to shoot at the ground the same distance away. What do I think of this statement? How do I feel about it?

_____

_____

_____

"The ancestor of every action is thought."

Ralph Waldo Emerson

13. "Many engage in wishful thinking – which by itself is without effect simply because the power factor is missing." What is the "power factor"?

_____

_____

_____

_____

14. Fill in the Blank: "Whatever you _____ your thoughts upon, or _____ _____ your imagination upon, that is what you _____."

15. Look around my home, office, space or room – what suggestions am I giving myself? What sort of reminders or thought provokers?

_____

_____

_____

16. I am bombarded with news, events, chaos, plans, other people's opinions, needs, ideas and demands of daily living. All of this along with my own desires, plans and opinions. As a result, I am sometimes scattered and my focus is diluted. In order to accurately impress the subconscious mind with my desires I must focus, I must concentrate on a single desire or suggestion. One of the best ways to do this is by using index cards as a reminder. In using this technique and in choosing my main desire, I must make sure it's something that feels good when I think about it, not something that feels impossible or unattainable. I will start small if necessary. And I will not think about HOW it will come about. I will leave that to the subconscious mechanism. Use the index card technique as described in the book.

Bonus: On my index cards, add the phrase, "I'm thankful and grateful for all the good things in my life." Repeat this at least 3 times daily and out loud is better.

17. The author has much to say about using repetition for consistent and persistent auto-suggestion. I am probably unconsciously doing this already. What do I usually say to myself? What are the repeated suggestions I hear and believe? Are they generally negative or positive?

_____

_____

_____

_____

_____

"Every thought we have is a tangible energy with the power to transform. A thought is not only a thing; a thought is a thing that influences other things."

Lynne McTaggart,
The Intention Experiment

Bonus: On the same or other index cards, add the phrase, "Day by day in every way I'm getting better, better and better." Repeat this at least 3 times a day and out loud is best.

18. "You must keep your subconscious mind fed at all times with positive thoughts so that their strong vibrations will ward off all negative and destructive thoughts from the outside." How can I do this? What's my plan?

_____

_____

_____

_____

19. Fill in the Blank: "Strange as it may sound, we usually get what we _____."

20. The author talks about the fact that we are all, to some degree, "hypnotized" by common, popular culture. In what ways do I see this in effect around me?

_____

_____

_____

_____

21. In what ways do I see it in my own life, beliefs and expectations?

_____

_____

_____

_____

_____

22. Who do I know that's a 'talker'? Who do I know that's a 'doer'?

_____

_____

_____

_____

23. How much do I believe in the power of believing? (1 being a little, 10 being a great deal.)

1-------------2-------------3-------------4-------------5-------------6-------------7-------------8-------------9-------------10

24. n this chapter, the author speaks much about how suggestion by repetition can be used to convince the subconscious mind. How is this different from any prior understanding I had of positive thinking?

_____

_____

_____

_____

25. What other thoughts or experiences did I have while reading this chapter?

_____

_____

_____

_____

_____

_____

_____

_____

_____

_____

_____

_____

_____

_____

_____

_____

_____

_____

_____

"This Creative Mechanism within you is impersonal. It will work automatically and impersonally to achieve goals of success and happiness, or unhappiness and failure, depending upon the goals which you yourself set for it."

Maxwell Maltz, M.D., *Psycho-Cybernetics*

Chapter 6
The Mirror Technique for Releasing the Subconscious

Chapter 6. The Mirror Technique for Releasing the Subconscious

1. "The toughest problem that confronts most people is a lack of money." Some people have a "money consciousness". They think wealth, abundance and prosperity. What are my predominant thoughts about money?

_____

_____

_____

2. How do I feel when I think those thoughts about money?

_____

_____

3. How did I feel when I read the story of the woman who, in 25 years, created her own business and financial success?

_____

_____

4. What about the story of the young druggist? What did I think of that?

_____

_____

_____

5. Consider that everything I see around me right now, every physical object, device, structure, product and thing was first an idea in someone's imagination. An idea followed by action. What great ideas have I had that I didn't act upon?

_____

_____

_____

6. Imagine what it would have been like to be raised the way J.A. Zehntbauer was – with a focus on the positive side of things and constant encouragement that I could do anything if I set my mind on it. How would that have changed my world view? How would that change my attitude?

_____

_____

_____

7. Fill in the Blanks: "If you do not _____ your own thoughts, then you will _____ the thoughts of the fellow who _____ his."

8. "Use your cards and your constant affirmations until belief in your goal becomes a vital part of you, and you feel it in your blood, your bones, and in every tissue of your body. See yourself actually doing the things you visualize, and it will all work out, because every thought held constantly and persistently sooner or later materializes after its kind."

   This is a deep belief! A trust, a knowingness. Do I believe in my dream like this?

   _____

   _____

   _____

9. Do I visualize my success "constantly and persistently"?

   _____

   _____

   _____

Bonus: Think, ponder or meditate on the statement "every thought held constantly and persistently sooner or later materializes after its kind".

10. Remember a time when I planned a trip, an outing, an event, cross country or to the grocery store, it doesn't matter. An art project, a haircut, clothes shopping or house cleaning it's all the same. Think about the mental process involved and how I see the end result before I begin.

    _____

    _____

    _____

11. Have I ever watched a 'Behind the Scenes' feature for a movie or TV show? Think about all the planning, visualizing, coordinating and dreaming that goes into all that! It started as an idea in someone's imagination. Watch some behind the scenes footage for a major production. What's my impression?

    _____

    _____

    _____

    _____

    _____

"Belief in great results is the driving force, the power behind all great books, plays, scientific discoveries. Belief in success is behind every successful business, church, and political organization.

Belief in success is the one basic, absolutely essential ingredient in successful people. Believe, really believe, you can succeed and you will."

David Schwartz, Ph.D,
The Magic of Thinking Big

12. Get in front of a mirror and try the mirror technique. Do it now! What do I want? How do I feel?

_____

_____

13. For the next 30 days use the mirror technique at least once a day and twice is better. What was my experience?

Day 1: _____

_____

_____

Day 2: _____

_____

_____

Day 3: _____

_____

_____

Day 4: _____

_____

_____

Day 5: _____

_____

_____

Day 6: _____

_____

_____

Day 7: _____

_____

_____

Day 8: _____

_____

_____

Day 9: _____

_____

_____

Day 10: _____

_____

_____

Day 11: _____

_____

_____

Day 12: _____

_____

_____

Day 13 _____

_____

_____

Day 14: _____

_____

_____

Day 15: _____

_____

_____

Day 16: _____

_____

_____

Day 17: _____

_____

_____

Day 18: _____

_____

_____

Day 19: _____

_____

_____

Day 20: _____

_____

_____

Day 21 _____

_____

_____

Day 22: _____

_____

_____

Day 23: _____

_____

_____

Day 24: _____

_____

_____

Day 25 _____

_____

_____

Day 26: _____

_____

_____

Day 27: _____

_____

_____

Day 28: _____

_____

_____

"Nothing stops you from realizing your objective save your failure to feel that you are already that which you wish to be, or that you are already in possession of the thing sought. Your subconscious gives form to your desires only when you feel your wish fulfilled."

Neville Goddard, *Feeling is the Secret*

Day 29 _____

_____

_____

Day 30: _____

_____

_____

Bonus: Write on the mirror with soap or tape a piece of paper somewhere I'll see it often with a positive message for myself.

14. Do I recognize my own intuition when it speaks?

_____

_____

15. Do I act on my intuition?

_____

_____

16. How does the author describe a "true hunch" as opposed to gambling or mere fancy?

_____

_____

17. "As long as you hold on to the mental picture of your idea and begin to develop it with action, nothing can stop you from succeeding, for **the subconscious mind never fails to obey any order given clearly and emphatically**." How do I see evidence of this in my life?

_____

_____

_____

_____

18. What thoughts do I hold that my subconscious accepts and acts upon?

_____

_____

_____

_____

"Therefore I say to you, whatever things you ask when you pray, believe that you receive them, and you will have them."

Mark 11:24

19. Throughout the book so far, no time line or expectation of quick manifestation is given. Can I hold on to the mental picture of my idea or dream without doubting or becoming impatient?

_____

_____

_____

_____

20. What other thoughts or experiences did I have while reading this chapter?

_____

_____

_____

_____

_____

_____

_____

_____

_____

_____

_____

_____

_____

_____

_____

_____

_____

_____

_____

_____

_____

Chapter 7
How to Project Your Thoughts

"We may imagine that thought can be kept secret, but it cannot; it rapidly crystallizes into habit, and habit solidifies into circumstance."

James Allen, *As a Man Thinketh*

Chapter 7. How to Project Your Thoughts

1. The author explains how valuable my initiative is for success. Look up the word 'initiative' in the dictionary. What does it mean?

_____

_____

_____

2. What can I do today, tomorrow, this week to develop the habit of initiative at work?

_____

_____

_____

3. Now apply that initiative anywhere and everywhere: what can I do at home, at school, in my business, in my relationships?

_____

_____

_____

_____

4. Fill in the Blank: "We all do best what _____ us."

5. What do I do that really absorbs my attention and interest?

_____

_____

_____

6. Who do I know who's dependable and reliable? Who isn't?

_____

_____

_____

7. Am I dependable and reliable?

_____

_____

"A man is but the product of his thoughts.
What he thinks, he becomes."

Mahatma Ghandi

8. Ok, that's what I think of me. Is it possible that others perceive me differently? How might someone else think of me in this area?

_____

_____

9. Take a good look at the relationships in my life: family, friends, enemies, coworkers, acquaintances and others. My interactions with people are always a reflection of my thoughts, of what I project mentally. What sorts of thoughts do I typically think of others and how do I see this reflected in my relationships?

_____

_____

_____

_____

10. The author says that a person who desires riches must go where riches are. Whatever it is I want, I must go to where it is, to be around the people who have it. What would be an example of this for me?

_____

_____

_____

_____

11. In accordance with the previous question, consider this: what sorts of books do I read? What do I watch? Who do I listen to?

_____

_____

_____

12. How much do I know about where I work? Take some time to research the people, duties and information for the 2 positions above mine. If this type of structure doesn't apply to me or my workplace, is there something I would like to be doing, somewhere I would like to be working? If so, research that.

_____

_____

_____

"Whether you have been aware of your thoughts in the past or not, now you are becoming aware. Right now, with the knowledge of The Secret, you are waking up from a deep sleep and becoming aware! Aware of the knowledge, aware of the law, aware of the power you have through your thoughts."

Rhonda Byrne, *The Secret*

13. Fill in the Blanks: "The more you read, the more your _____ is _____, and if you are a person of _____, the more your efforts are _____."

_____

_____

14. What types of books do I read?

_____

_____

15. The author briefly mentions idea association, saying it is of great value and should be cultivated by everyone. Why? Why is this information inserted here in the book?

_____

_____

16. "**The world accepts you as you appear to be**." How do I 'package' myself?

_____

_____

17. Based on how I'm dressed, how do I feel about myself? How am I treated?

_____

_____

18. Write about a time when my dress, my packaging, my appearance, gave me a sense of power and confidence.

_____

_____

Bonus: Dig a little deeper and research Theos Bernard and *Penthouse of the Gods*. Thoughts:

_____

_____

_____

_____

_____

_____

19. Have I ever felt, or imagined I felt, my own energy or aura or that of another person?

_____

_____

_____

_____

20. Recall a time or two when I've noticed or felt the vibration or atmosphere in a house, room or office. What was it like? How did I know?

_____

_____

_____

_____

21. Am I generally wishy-washy and hesitant to decide? Think of something in my life right now, big or small, that needs a decision. Now decide. Yes, it can be that simple.

_____

_____

_____

_____

22. What are my thoughts on the phenomenon of telepathy?

_____

_____

_____

_____

Bonus: Try the "Leave now" experiment on someone. What was my experience?

_____

_____

_____

_____

_____

23. When's the last time I thought of an "original" idea and then saw it pop up somewhere else?

_____

_____

_____

_____

24. This chapter is titled, "How to project your thoughts". Go back through the chapter to find and list the ways, methods and means to project my thoughts.

_____

_____

_____

_____

_____

_____

_____

_____

25. What other thoughts or experiences did I have while reading this chapter?

_____

_____

_____

_____

_____

_____

_____

_____

_____

_____

_____

Chapter 8
Women and the Science of Belief

"Whatever you do you need courage. Whatever course you decide upon, there is always someone to tell you that you are wrong. There are always difficulties arising that tempt you to believe your critics are right...

"Do the thing and you will have the power."

Ralph Waldo Emerson

Chapter 8. Women and the Science of Belief

1. The Magic of Believing was first published in 1948 and of course, so much has changed since then. In what ways has the world changed for women? How has it changed for men?

_____

_____

_____

_____

_____

_____

2. What woman of today do I admire for her accomplishments or contribution?

_____

_____

_____

_____

3. Fill in the Blank: "_____ creates its _____ in fact; and affords unmistakable proof that often events are influenced by our very great _____."

4. What do I think of the story of Opal Whitely? Do a little digging to learn more of the facts and details.

_____

_____

_____

_____

5. The author says that in many instances, when a prophecy or foretelling of the future is given, the power of suggestion works in the individual's subconscious mind to make the prophecy a reality and produce the outcome. How can I use this to my advantage?

_____

_____

_____

_____

_____

"Continuous effort – not strength or intelligence – is the key to unlocking your potential."

Sir Winston Churchill

6. Do I have enough conviction like the women discussed in this chapter? What do I believe in strongly enough to **persist**?

_____

_____

_____

_____

_____

7. Fill in the Blank: "She, too, was fought at every turn, but being inspired with the _____ of the destiny which she thought was hers, obstacles meant nothing to her."

Bonus: Of all the women's stories mentioned, choose one or two that inspire me, that resonate with me, that stir something inside me. Now delve deeper into the stories of those women. What did I learn, what did I get out of it?

_____

_____

_____

_____

_____

_____

_____

_____

8. What does Angela Lansbury say about how to use the suggestibility of the subconscious?

_____

_____

_____

_____

9. How did I feel while reading these stories of accomplishments and dreams turned into reality?

_____

_____

_____

_____

10. How are "wonderful results" brought about? Explain this in my own words.

_____

_____

_____

_____

_____

11. Fill in the Blanks: "The only thing you need is the power of believing -- _____,

_____ and _____."

12. What other thoughts or experiences did I have while reading this chapter?"

_____

_____

_____

_____

_____

_____

_____

_____

_____

_____

_____

_____

_____

_____

_____

_____

_____

_____

Chapter 9
Belief Makes Things Happen

"The power to *think* as you wish to *think* is the only power over which you have absolute control."

Napoleon Hill,
The Law of Success in 16 Lessons

Chapter 9. Belief Makes Things Happen

1. How do I think animals communicate?

_____

_____

Bonus: Dig into the Facial Sight project and Dr. Jacob Levine of Old Farms school in Connecticut. What did I learn?

_____

_____

_____

2. The author gives several examples of people using their "thought power" to influence others. What's my experience with this thought power?

_____

_____

3. How do my strongest thoughts affect those around me?

_____

_____

4. The author tells of a husband and wife who came to see him. The husband says, "Don't get me wrong. I am not religious in an orthodox sense, and what I talk about is not goody-goody stuff, but an exact science. What we think or contemplate develops into reality. We radiate our thoughts, perhaps unconsciously, to others, and we affect them. We give forth vibrations of dislike or hatred which we engender in ourselves – and, bingo, they come right back and floor us. All one needs to do is to study and understand the law of cause and effect, and it all becomes plain." Re-write or re-state his words in my own:

_____

_____

_____

_____

_____

_____

"Everybody in the world is seeking happiness – and there is one sure way to find it. That is by controlling your thoughts. Happiness doesn't depend on outward conditions. It depends on inner conditions."

Dale Carnegie,
How To Win Friends & Influence People

5. What DO I think of the "evidence" of telepathy and thought power?

_____

_____

_____

Bonus: Do the colored paper experiment with two other people; ideally, people who are open to the experiment and not "scoffers". What was our experience?

_____

_____

_____

6. Fill in the Blanks: "Always remember that _____ is a power operating _____ or _____, depending upon the end to which it is employed."

7. Who decides the end to which it is employed?

_____

_____

8. Dr. Rhine and other experimenters concluded that thoughts or suggestions from other people could influence and affect the ability of the person attempting telepathy or other experiments. It can therefore be concluded that other people's thoughts and beliefs influence me and my own thinking. What outside suggestions do I allow in?

_____

_____

_____

9. How can I further control the outside suggestions that influence me?

_____

_____

_____

10. In my own words, re-write the author's definition and explanation of happiness.

_____

_____

_____

_____

11. What did Marcus Aurelius Antoninus say about opinion?

_____

_____

_____

12. What do I think of that idea?

_____

_____

_____

13. The author talks about taking control of our power and ability to think. I do this by fixing my attention, controlling my focus, consciously choosing what to think about and thereby creating new habits and patterns of thinking. I want to be at cause over the effect that my own thinking has in my life. How do I do this?

_____

_____

_____

_____

14. What is meant by "positive creative thought"?

_____

_____

_____

15. What other thoughts or experiences did I have while reading this chapter?

_____

_____

_____

_____

_____

_____

_____

Chapter 10
Gold diggers: Hitting Pay Dirt!

"Use your mind to form a mental image of what you want, and to hold that vision with faith and purpose, and use your will to keep your mind working in the Right Way... Since belief is all important, it behooves you to guard your thoughts; and as your beliefs will be shaped to a very great extent by the things you observe and think about, it is important that you should command your attention."

Wallace Wattles,
The Science of Getting Rich

Chapter 10. Gold diggers: Hitting Pay Dirt!

1. What have I learned about the power of suggestion and how to use it to my advantage?

_____

_____

_____

_____

2. Have I decided what I most want in life? Do I know what my dream is?

_____

_____

_____

3. How often do I visualize the attainment of my dreams and goals?

_____

_____

4. Does it feel *real* to me, like I'm living it now?

_____

_____

5. On a scale from 1 to 10, how much do I *believe* I can be the person I want to be? ? (1 being a little, 10 being a great deal.)

    1-------------2-------------3-------------4-------------5-------------6-------------7-------------8-------------9-------------10

6. On a scale from 1 to 10, how much do I *believe* I can achieve whatever it is I want to achieve? (1 being a little, 10 being a great deal.)

    1-------------2-------------3-------------4-------------5-------------6-------------7-------------8-------------9-------------10

7. How do I feel when I think about what I want?

_____

_____

_____

_____

_____

"The mind works like a garden. Everyone knows if you plant beans you won't raise potatoes – you will raise beans. Obviously you don't plant a bean to raise a bean – you plant a bean to raise *lots* of beans. Between planting and harvest there is a tremendous increase in the number of beans.

That's the way the mind works. Whatever you plant in the mind is going to come up – multiplied. Plant *a* negative or *a* positive and you reap in multitudes because between planting and harvest, imagination enters the picture and multiplies the result."

Zig Ziglar, *See You at the Top*

8. Analyze how my beliefs are acted out in my life as compared to how others' beliefs are acted out in theirs. How do our beliefs influence our actions?

_____

_____

9. How has this information changed the way I view the beliefs and opinions of others?

_____

_____

10. How has this information changed the way I view my own beliefs and opinions?

_____

_____

11. Are my beliefs and opinions frozen or open to adjustment?

_____

_____

12. Have I been using the mirror technique? If so, what have I experienced? If not, why not?

_____

_____

13. What are my thoughts on the power of believing?

_____

_____

_____

14. What is the biggest 'ah-ha!' moment I had while going through this process?

_____

_____

_____

15. How did that new understanding change the way I think; the way I act; the way I speak?

_____

_____

_____

_____

16. What will I do next to keep myself moving forward? What book will I read? What event will I attend? What habit will I change or create? What friendships will I cultivate?

_____

_____

_____

_____

_____

_____

17. Choose a statement or two from this book that resonated with me, impacted me, or caused me to pause and consider. Write that statement or idea on a card and put it in my wallet, pocket or purse. For two weeks, read it every time I touch or see it. What statements will I choose?

_____

_____

_____

_____

18. What did I like best about the book, _The Magic of Believing_ and the workbook process?

_____

_____

_____

19. What did I get out of the book and the workbook process?

_____

_____

_____

20. Think of how I felt before I started this journey of digging a little deeper. In what ways do I feel differently now? In what ways do I think differently? What has changed in my life since then?

_____

_____

_____

_____

_____

21. Having finished the book and this in-depth study, how would I write an introduction or foreword to *The Magic of Believing*? Pretend that I'm writing the foreword that will go out with the next printing of the book. What will I say? Write it now:

_____

_____

_____

_____

_____

_____

_____

_____

_____

_____

_____

_____

_____

_____

_____

22. How much do I believe in the **power of believing**? (1 being a little, 10 being a great deal.)

1-------------2-------------3-------------4-------------5-------------6-------------7-------------8-------------9-------------10

"The object of all life is development; and everything that lives has an inalienable right to all the development it is capable of attaining. The very best thing you can do for the whole world is to make the most of yourself."

Wallace Wattles,
The Science of Getting Rich

Afterword

Congratulations! You've come a long way.

I recommend reading the book again, noticing how you interact with the information differently, feel differently and pick up something new. As a matter of fact, you'll pick up something new every time you read it.

Keep moving forward on your journey and remember, the only way to get better is to *get better!* The only way to develop a skill is to *develop it*. The only way to change or create a habit is to *change it!* This means that it's a choice. It's a choice in every little decision we make.

Never stop learning!

"What you are looking for is creative control of your own focus... Life is not about tomorrow, it is about right now. Life is about how you are currently molding the Energy!"

Abraham, *Ask and It Is Given*

Recommended Reading List:

The Magic of Thinking Big by David Schwartz

As a Man Thinketh by James Allen

Ask and It is Given by Esther and Jerry Hicks.

Any and all books by Esther and Jerry Hicks.

The Law of Success in 16 Lessons by Napoleon Hill

Think and Grow Rich by Napoleon Hill

The Science of Getting Rich by Wallace Wattles

It Works: The Famous Little Red Book That Makes Your Dreams Come True! by R.H. Jarrett

You Were Born Rich by Bob Proctor

Psycho-Cybernetics by Maxwell Maltz

The Power of Positive Thinking by Norman Vincent Peale

The Secret by Rhonda Byrne

Acres of Diamonds by Russell Conwell

How to Win Friends and Influence People by Dale Carnegie

The Game of Work by Charles Coonradt

How to Have Power and Confidence in Dealing with People by Les Giblin

See You at the Top by Zig Ziglar

How I Raised Myself from Failure to Success in Selling by Frank Bettger

The Awesome Science of Luck – Your Guide to Winning All the Time by Peter Ragnar

Current research on the science of mind and life:

The Field: The Quest for the Secret Force of the Universe by Lynne McTaggart

The Intention Experiment: Using Your Thoughts to Change Your Life and the World by Lynne McTaggart

The Bond: Connecting Through the Space Between Us by Lynne McTaggart

Morphic Resonance: The Nature of Formative Causation; 4th Edition, Revised and Expanded Edition of *A New Science of Life* by Rupert Sheldrake

Science Set Free: 10 Paths to New Discovery by Rupert Sheldrake

Unbelievable: Investigations into Ghosts, Poltergeists, Telepathy and Other Unseen Phenomena from the Duke Parapsychology Laboratory by Stacy Horn

Additional Resource

The Global Information Network:
www.globalinformationnetwork.com and http://bekah.myginclub.com

Notes

Notes

Notes

"All the water in the world cannot sink a ship unless it gets on the inside of it. All the worry and anxiety and frustration and jealousy in the world cannot sink a person unless it gets on the inside of your mind.

So how do you keep worry and anxiety and frustration and jealousy outside your mind?

You keep your mind so full of hopes and dreams and love and understanding that there's no room for it to creep in."

Ed Foreman

Notes

Notes